Shari Harpaz

Molly
Find Your
Voice

First Edition Book, 2023

978-1-957506-76-0 – paperback
978-1-957506-77-7 – hardback

Published by Skinny Brown Dog Media Atlanta, GA
www.skinnybrowndogmedia.com
Distributed by Skinny Brown Dog Media

Dedication

To Casey - May you forever follow your dreams and reach for the stars, find your passions and believe in yourself. You've got this!

Molly stood frozen in place as she stared at the calendar on her refrigerator. The Holiday Talent Show auditions were during music class tomorrow and she was very worried.

As she stared at tomorrow's date, she imagined herself on stage as a big microphone opened its mouth to swallow her head.

Molly loved to sing and she knew she was a good singer. She always performed at home and sang as she twirled down the street.

Her music teacher often praised her talent and during her lessons they had even recorded videos of the songs Molly had written. But Molly had never been on a stage in front of an audience before.

"Mommy," Molly said. "What if I mess up? What if I forget the words? What if other kids laugh at me," she asked nervously.

Molly's mom held her close. "Sweetheart, it's normal to feel nervous when trying something new. Did you know that even professional singers feel that way before they get on stage." "Really? They do?," Molly questioned.

"They sure do. Do you want to learn a funny trick that your grandma taught me?" her mom said with a grin. "When you get on stage, imagine that everyone in the audience has turned into... dancing puppies!"

Molly giggled as she hugged her mom. That night, she peacefully drifted off to sleep dreaming of a theater filled with puppies.

The next morning, Molly's stomach felt like frogs were leaping inside. She was too nervous to eat her favorite breakfast. Molly couldn't think of anything other than the auditions.

As Molly got to school, her mom said, "Remember, fear might sit ON you sometimes, but it's not all of you. The feeling won't last forever. You've got this my brave, kind girl."

Molly was thinking about her mom's words as she entered her classroom. She saw Julia, Drew, Emma, and Ben huddled together, chatting and laughing.

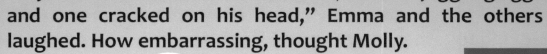

"My dad said that when he was a kid, he tried juggling eggs and one cracked on his head," Emma and the others laughed. How embarrassing, thought Molly.

Just then, their teacher, Ms. Lopez, told the class to get ready for music. Molly lingered as she watched all the other kids excitedly line up.

At the back of the line, Julia whispered to Molly, "I'm really nervous." Molly looked at her with surprise, "You are? So am I."

They smiled at each other, relieved to not be alone with those worried feelings. Then they hurried to catch up with the rest of the class.

The children took turns showing off their talents on stage. Some friends danced, some told jokes, a few juggled (with balls not eggs), and others sang.

Molly's mind felt split in two. One half wanted to go on stage and sing her favorite song, while the other half wanted to hide. It felt like a tug of war in her mind and she wasn't sure which half would win.

Molly it's your turn," called Mr. Potter, the music teacher.

Molly tried to stand up but her body wouldn't budge. She felt like she was glued to her seat. Her legs were as heavy as cement blocks.

In what felt like 3 hours, but probably was just 15 seconds, she finally made it on to the stage.

Molly stood at the microphone wishing puppies would magically appear in the auditorium seats. The music began to play. Molly closed her eyes, opened her mouth and...nothing happened. Her voice had disappeared.

Molly ran off the stage, holding back tears, and bumped into her teacher. "Molly, it's ok. You can try again later if you want," Ms Lopez tried to comfort her.

Suddenly, Molly heard a sound coming from behind the stage curtain. She ran towards the curtain but didn't see anyone.

Then she heard something again. The sound was coming from the costume room. Molly could recognize it anywhere; it was HER VOICE! Molly leaped into the room and SNAP! She grabbed her VOICE and put it back in her mouth where it belonged!

Molly walked over to Mr. Potter. "Um, excuse me Mr. Potter. Can I try again?" He smiled, gave her a thumbs up and started the music

Molly tightly squeezed the microphone, opened her mouth to sing. But, oh no, her voice ran out AGAIN!

Molly sat down exasperated. She didn't want her fear to win, but she didn't know what else to do.

Ms. Lopez and Julia walked towards her as they called her name. It was too late. School was over for the day.

Her mom saw tears in Molly's eyes as she left school. Ms. Lopez explained that they had just come from the auditions and Molly was very disappointed.

When they got home, Molly sat snuggling her dog Rosy, hoping it would help her feel better. "Mommy, I couldn't do it. I tried to sing on stage and my voice disappeared when I opened my mouth." Rosy was doing her best to lick away the tears rolling down Molly's cheeks. "I even tried a second time and it happened again."

"Oh sweetheart," her mom said as she gently kissed her head. "You know what? I'm really proud of you, Molly. You were so brave. You were scared but you tried. And not just once, but twice." Molly nestled closer in the comfort of her mom's arms.

After a while, her mom said, "I need to go to make dinner. Do you want to help?" Molly wanted to be alone so she went to her room. She tried to color but her mind drifted thinking about her mom's words.

Was it true? Had brave really won the tug of war even though no sound had come out of her mouth?

That night, Molly dreamt that she was on stage, wearing a beautiful sparkly gown and her favorite Brave/Kind necklace. She sang louder than ever before to an audience full of dancing puppies

Molly woke up with a big stretch and sang "It's a new day," a special song she and her mom had made up. It helped her start the day with positivity.

"It's a new day and what you gonna say..hooray!

We're gonna dance the worries away."

Molly was excited to run into school and see her friends. She couldn't wait to tell them about her dream with the dancing puppy audience.

"Good morning, Ms. Lopez. Do you think I could go see Mr. Potter and audition again? I'm feeling extra brave and ready this morning." Ms. Lopez nodded, "Of course you can. Would you like to take a friend with you?"

Molly and Julia skipped down the hall. "I can do it, I've got this," Molly mumbled as she made her way to audition.

"Hi Mr. Potter. I'm ready today. Can I please try again?"

The music started, Molly opened her mouth, and her beautiful voice filled the theater.

Molly was so proud of herself. She had done it! She had shaken her fear off and couldn't wait to perform at the Holiday Show.

That day, Molly truly found her voice and nothing would take it away from her!

Happy

Surprised

Quiet

Scared

Sad

Silly

Curious

Excited

Mad

Printed in the USA
CPSIA information can be obtained
at www.ICGtesting.com
LVHW072351261023
761974LV00018B/254